HONESTY
is the
BEST
POLICY

Cecile A. Nelson

THE AUTHOR

Cecile A. Nelson is a native of Kingston, Jamaica. She currently resides in Fort Lauderdale, Florida with her husband. A member of the International Society of Poets – she currently has poems published in an anthology called "The Space Between". Her favorite pastime of writing journals and novels began at an early age, but she was too shy to go to the publishing level until now. Her passion for writing children's books, was rejuvenated by her niece Gabrielle, on a recent trip to her homeland. The two week trip has given her enough information to write several books – not to mention all the material she had. Her first novel –"**A TWIST TO LOVE**" was released in May 2010. She is currently working on the Sequel (CONQUERING LIONESS) which will be released this Summer.

ACKNOWLEDGEMENTS

With the help of my dear husband "Ras Mike".... I have been able to finish this book.... I have been under a "writer's block hold" for many months, and he pushed me to snap out of it.

Many thanks to all the people in my life... my friends, my readers and even my critics. Without you folks --- I am a lost soul.

Children are the most precious people in the world...

We all are children

- therefore.....

WE ALL ARE SPECIAL !!

One Love,

Cecile

PREFACE

I like the fact that that I am able to relate to children of all ages. It is important to me that they not only read, but understand what they read.

Some instances are in pictorial form… because most of us like to have visuals. Visuals enable us to understand and allow things to sink in.

The questions on this story, are geared to have us remember the salient (most noticeable or important) points.

It is my intention that : no matter the age of the person who reads this book…. Each person will remember that "HONESTY IS THE BEST POLICY !"

*** honesty is …. the quality of being fair and truthful

"Joshua, It is 6:45 A.M!!"

" Why are you still here?"

My mother was shouting at me from the top of the stairs, because I was going to be late for school. Usually I would leave home at 6:30 A.M. to give myself enough time to get to the schoolyard on time. This particular morning for some reason – I was wasting time, doing nothing.

"I'm leaving now Mom, see you later and have a good day." I said locking our front door behind me.

"Thank you my son, you do the same. Be careful "

Because I was off to a late start, I had to walk alone. My friend Timothy and his sister Tina had already passed the house. I knew, because I had heard his whistle a few minutes earlier. By my calculation, I would get to school just in time for the first bell, so technically – I wouldn't be late.

As I went around the bend at the end of my street, I looked down towards the curb and what I saw made my heart leap. Lying on the ground next to a shiny black BMW, was a fifty dollar bill. Moving closer to it, I looked around to make sure no one was looking. With a quick motion, I snatched up the money, stuffed it into my jacket pocket and continued on my journey. It was not a very pleasant walk. It was as if my mother was walking with me, as I heard her voice saying "Thou shalt not steal." Yet and still I ignored the voice – I had money in my pocket which made me feel bigger than life.

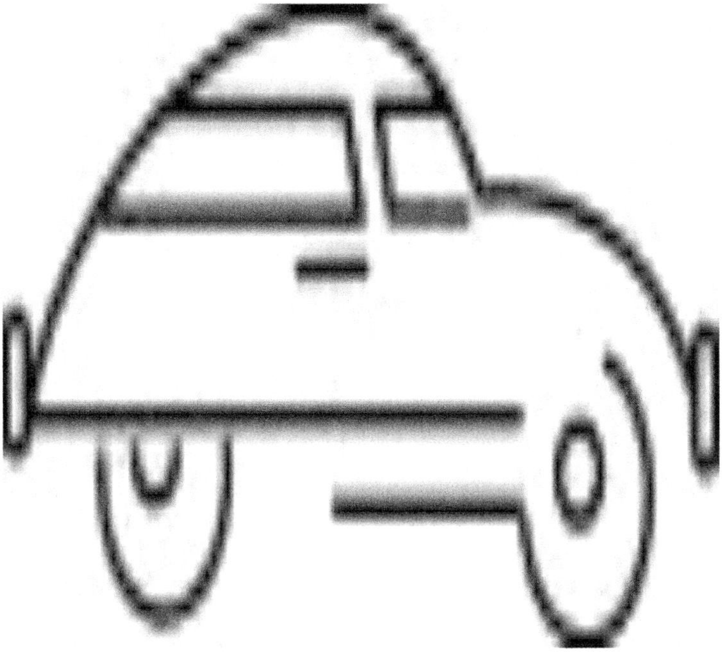

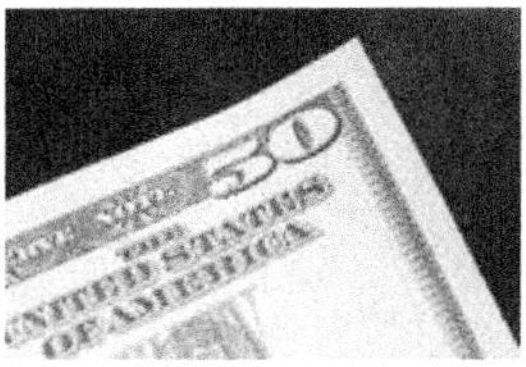

When I got to school and opened the door to my classroom, just as I thought – the first bell was rung by the principal who welcomed us back from the three day holiday weekend. I did not tell anyone about the money for fear they would tell the teacher. Instead I walked around school with my chest puffed up because I was rich.

At lunch time, I sat in my usual seat with my friends, but I couldn't help daydreaming of all the games I could buy on the weekend with this money. It was so bad that my friends were talking to me and I didn't hear a word they were saying.

" Joshua, did you hear anything we just said?" Timothy asked.

"N-O " ... I stuttered when I realized I really hadn't heard a single word.

"I was asking if you want to go to the arcade after school"

"No, not today, I have to go straight home." I replied quickly.

The bell sounded for the end of lunch. We cleared our places at the table and filed back to our classroom, for the beginning of fourth period. The intercom sounded shortly after we got settled and it was the principal telling us that we needed to go to the auditorium to listen to a guest speaker. So, we gathered up our belongings and filed into the auditorium with our teacher.

The speaker was introduced to us a Mr. Moon, a teacher from Boston who was going around to various schools with a message to young people. He was a tall man with big saucer looking eyes,

and big teeth like those of a beaver. I was not really in the mood to listen to him but I really had no choice in the matter. His first few words made my eyes pop open with fear.

"Good afternoon students, I am Mr. Moon and I would like to talk to you about HONESTY!"

I gained sudden interest. My mind raced back to the events of the morning. How coincidental that this man would be here to talk about honesty. He told us that we must not lie to anyone and that we must always be responsible and honest enough to return things when they don't belong to us.

"How does he know?" I muttered as I shook in my seat.

Instantly, I felt uncomfortable. As Mr. Moon finished his speech, my mind was made up to return the money to the owner of the car, on my way home, The rest of the day was a complete blur for me. We were instructed to remain in the auditorium and read our reading books, as there was only one hour left before dismissal.

Instead of reading, I was thinking about how I was going to return the money. The questions flooded my head one after the other. Should I drop it back where I found it? Maybe I should take it to the person who owns the car. My mind had already absorbed the fact that the right thing to do was return the money. The big question was – HOW. I was totally confused.

Finally the bell rang, and we all filed out of the auditorium. School was officially out, and I had a task to perform. Timothy and Tina were waiting for me at the school gate. When I spotted them, I had to think of something to tell them so they would walk without me.

"Hey guys, go on without me today, I'm stopping by the library before going home."

"Alright buddy" Timothy said.

"You know we would go with you, but Mom would have a fit if we were late."

"That's ok, see you all tomorrow then."

LIBRARY

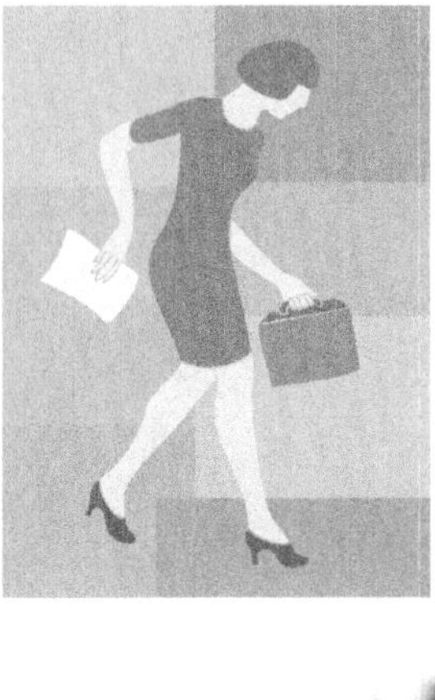

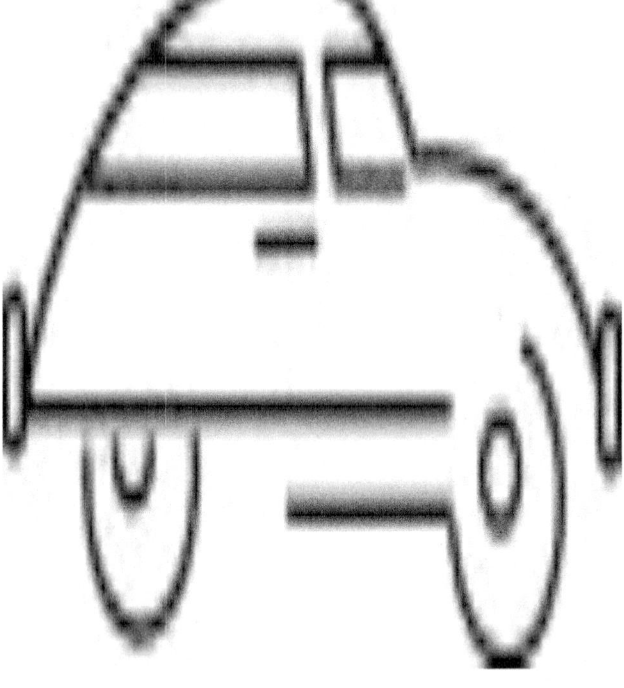

Fifteen minutes later when I knew they were out of range, I started heading for home. Approaching the curb where I picked up the money, I looked up just in time to see a woman opening the car door. My heart started pounding and my knees were shaking. I recognized the woman as Miss Lowe the school librarian, who also knew who my mother is. I knew they were not friends, but they had exchanged occasional hello's. She would definitely tell my mother and in turn, mother would punish me for years to come. That was a frightening thought.

"No way am I going to that woman." I muttered to myself with a shaky voice.

Unable to stop walking in her direction, it was as if I were in a trance. Head swirling with opening statements, I was staring at Miss Lowe and finally she looked up and saw me staring and shaking.

"Little boy, are you alright?"

"Yes Ma'am."

"B-U-T, B-U-T."

"What is it Young man?" she asked

Without looking at her, I started to explain my plight.

"Well, I, Well – this morning I picked up a fifty dollar bill that was on the ground by your tire. "

"I just want to return it, as I know was wrong of me to take it in the first place."

As I stretched out my hand to place the money in her hand, Miss Lowe looked back at me and smiled.

"Oh thank you little man, you are really an honest fellow."

Without waiting for her to ask any more questions, I backed away from her.

You're welcome Ma'am."

Hurriedly I made my way home. I knew that enough time had passed, and I should have been home long ago. Mom would be furious, and I would have to explain everything to her. Boy what a mess I was in. Getting closer to the house, I could see mom standing on the front porch.

"Oh Noooooo !" I said out loud.

"What a mess I created."

My mother wasted no time. As soon as she saw that it was me she started walking towards me.

"Young man, why are you so late?"

My heart skipped a few beats. She called me young man. Without giving me a chance to respond, she kept talking.

"Mr. Hall down the street saw you pick up some money from beside Miss Lowe's car this morning."

"Is that so Jati?" She asked softly.

With that tone of voice, and the fact that she called me by my nickname,I knew that she already knew the entire story and she was not as angry with me as I thought.

"Mom" I began speaking.

"Where is the money now son?"

"Mom, I returned the money to the lady who owns the car."

"While I was walking home, I saw her by her car and I gave it back to her."

"I know that too young man."

I held down my head and breathed a sigh of relief. Things could have been much worse if I had kept that money for myself.

"I just wanted to see how honest you are, and I am glad you reconsidered and gave it back."

"Come sit on the chair with me." She told me patting the seat next to her.

"My son, always remember one thing – Honesty is the best policy!"

That was the extent of what she had to say to me. She placed her arms around me, we got up and went inside the house.

I had surely learned my lesson today.

SELF TEST ~~~

In your opinion, was Joshua's action morally incorrect?

Would you have been bold enough to take the money?

Would you have returned it to the owner?

If you had done what Joshua did, and your mother found out. What would your mother have done?

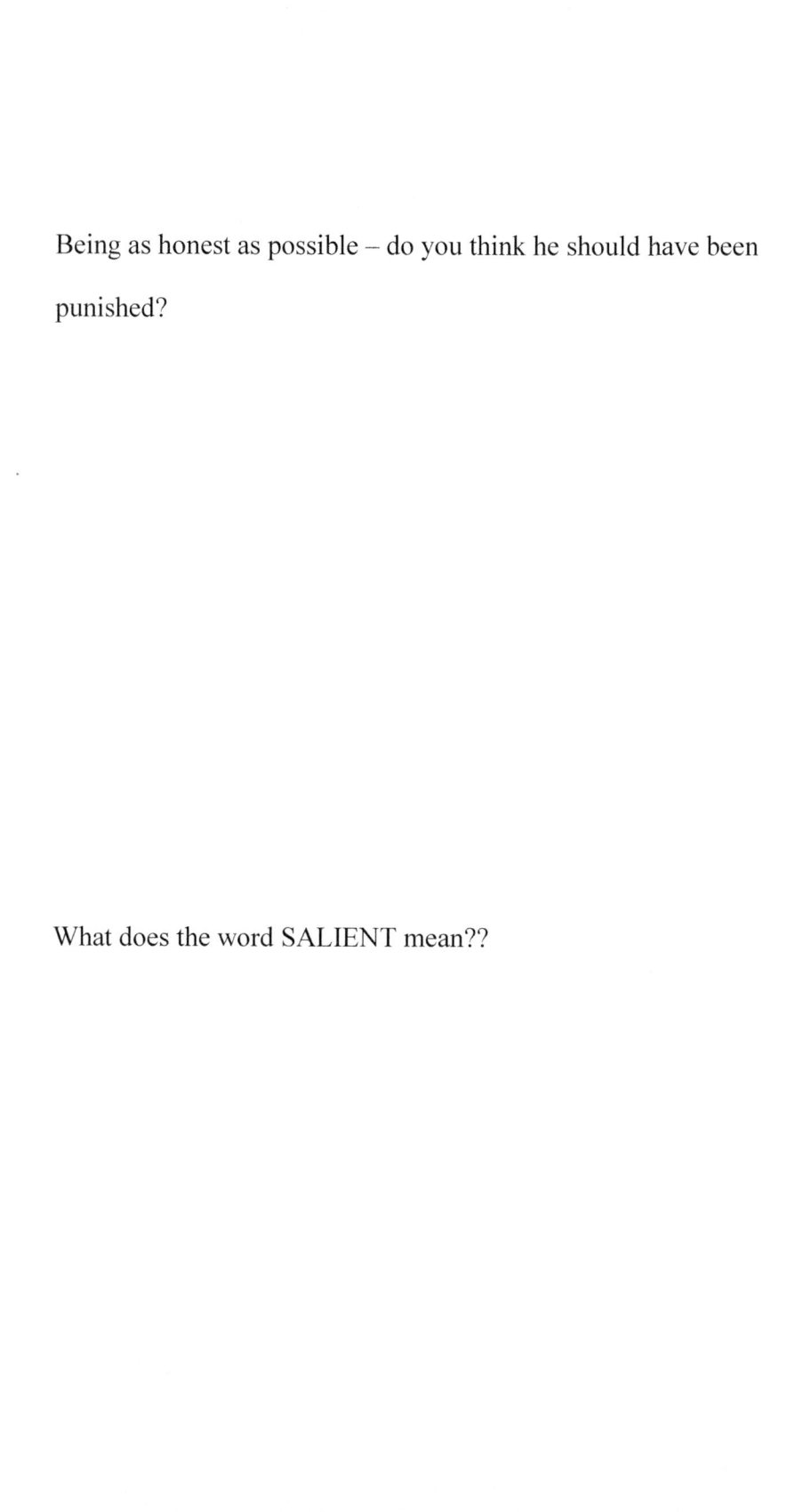

Being as honest as possible – do you think he should have been punished?

What does the word SALIENT mean??

Did this book help you ? if so… how?

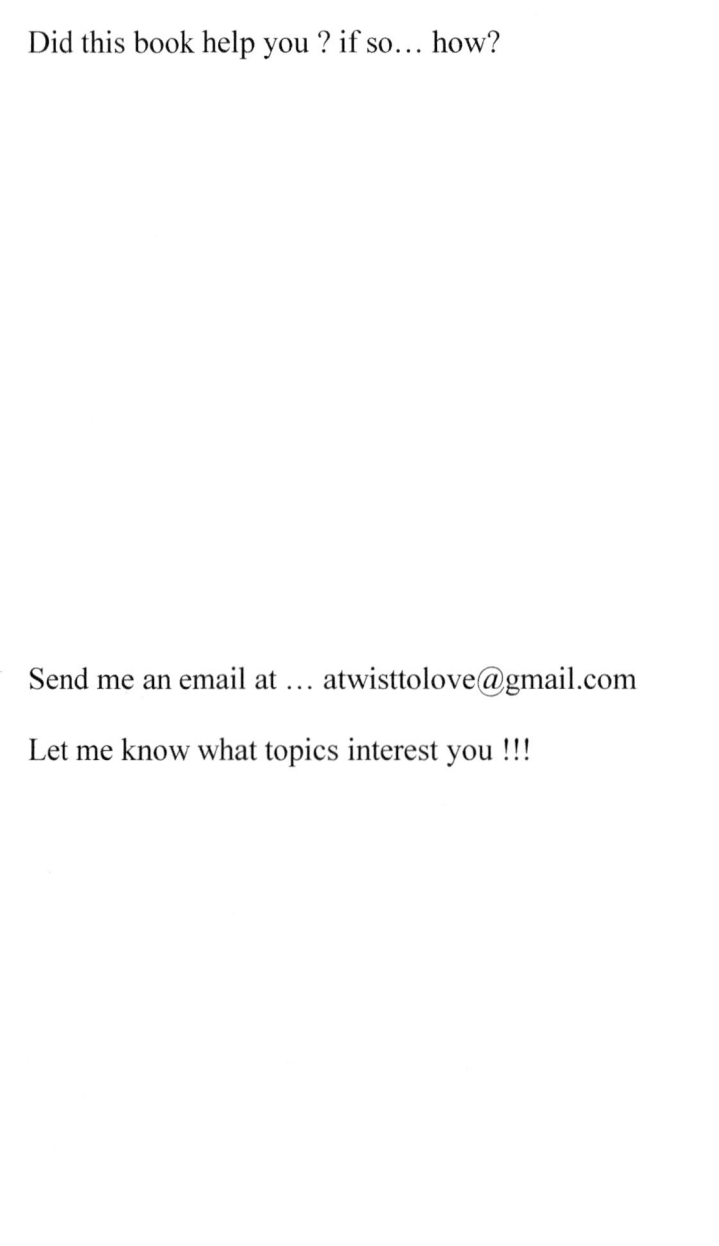

Send me an email at … atwisttolove@gmail.com

Let me know what topics interest you !!!